MY **MOOD** BOOK

make believe ideas

WHAT'S INSIDE?

Mood DICTIONARY

This dictionary is your mood guide.
Choose an icon and let it do the talking!

 angelic

 angry

 bashful

 best friends

 confused

 cool

 disappointed

 dizzy

 excited

 flattered

 frustrated

 geeky

 happy

 hungry

 love

 overjoyed

 overwhelmed

 relieved

 sad

 sarcastic

 scared

 secret

 shocked

 sick

 silly

 sleepy

 smiley

 stressed

 tears of laughter

 uncertain

 unhappy

 unimpressed

 upset

 witty

 worried

boom

 excited

 good

 peace

 strong

 thank you

 celebration

 hair flick

 massage

 no deal

 princess

 question

 boy

 family

 friends

 girl

 grandma

 grandpa

 man

 funny robot

 heard something funny

 said something funny

 saw something funny

 happy

 kisses

 love

 sad

 tears of joy

apple

 banana

 burger

 cake

 cherries

 chocolate bar

 cookie

 cupcake

 donut

 fries

 grapes

 ice cream

 lemon

 lollipop

 pear

 pineapple

 pizza

 popcorn

 strawberry

 sweet treats

 watermelon

 pear

 pineapple

 pizza

 popcorn

 strawberry

 sweet treats

WEATHER

 cloudy

 hot

 lightning

 rain

 rainbow

 raining

snowing

storm

sunny

thunderstorm

moon

sun

PRETTY THINGS

bow

butterfly

crown

diamond

lips

love letter

mermaid

mirror

perfume

pink cup

shell

star

stars

umbrella

unicorn

GLASSES

PLANTS

BAGS

CUTE ANIMALS

bear   bee   bunny   chick

chicken   dolphin   duck   elephant

fish   flamingo   frog   hatching chick

kitten   koala   ladybug   lion

mouse   octopus   panda   paw prints

pig   pug   puppy   snake

spider   tiger   turtle   whale

birthday

 bowling

 camera

 clothes shopping

 cycling

 dancing

 days out

 dinner

 drawing

 dress up

 driving

 eating

 exercise

 funfair

 games

 gaming

 good idea

 guitar

 hairbrush

 vacation

 jogging

 laptop

 lipstick

 makeup

 music

 nail polish

 painting

 painting nails

 party time

 playing music

 reading

 running

 shoe shopping

 singing

 special occasion

 sports

 summer vacation

 television

 tennis

 traveling

 waiting

 winning

MY moods

Circle three 😊 🍕 😣 that best describe
your feelings in these different situations.

Flying on a **plane**

Dinner with your family

A day on the beach with your **besties**

Your first day at a new **school**

Rehearsals for a **play**

A sleepover with your **besties**

Saying **sorry**

Saying **thank you**

Winning a running race at school

Waking up **early**

Listening to your favorite **song**

Performing in front of an audience

Getting a new **puppy**

Hiking with your **family**

Going to the **dentist**

Learning a new **language**

The first day of **summer**

Going to the **ZOO**

Celebrating your **birthday**

12

Finishing your science **homework**

Daydreaming

Making a new **friend**

Cheering for your team

Achieving your personal best in **sports**

Things that make you **smile** when you're **sad**

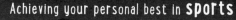

Running for a bus

Feeling **sick**

Studying for a **big test**

Swimming with **dolphins**

Spending time with your **grandparents**

13

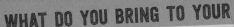

friendship group?

What role do you play in your friendship group? Take this test to find out.

Read the scenarios below. Choose your response and circle the letter next to it. When you are finished, count up your choices and turn to the next page to find out your role.

1 Which part of planning a party do you enjoy the most?

A making and sending invitations

B choosing the music and creating a playlist

C planning the games, activities, and surpises

D deciding who to invite

2 It's Monday morning and you're ready for school, but you still have 15 minutes to spare. Do you . . .

A make sure you've got the correct books for that day?

B watch some TV?

C wait in the car? You're itching to get going.

D make the most of the time to organize your planner?

3 Your parents have finally agreed to get you the pet you've always wanted. What do you do first?

A Write a list of everything your new pet will need: bed, toys, food . . . there's just so much!

B Daydream about all the fun you're going to have with your new pet.

C Call your friends to spread the news – you can't contain your excitement!

D Sit down with your parents and discuss it. A pet requires a lot of responsibility and time.

4 Which of these activities sounds the most appealing?

A redecorating your bedroom

B going to a theme park

C playing sports

D writing stories or poems

5 What do you find the most annoying?

A messy bedrooms

B boring movies

C when you're on the losing team

D making quick decisions

6 Your friends are trying to decide what to do on the weekend. Do you . . .

A take control and suggest some great ideas?

B let the group decide?

C suggest that you all think of ideas, and then vote on the best one?

D help think of new ideas by remembering all of the fun things you've done together in the past?

7 It's the last week of summer. What do you do first?

A Plan a trip to the stores to buy some school essentials.

B Throw an end-of-summer sleepover and invite all your friends.

C Get excited about the new projects you'll be working on at school.

D Create a memory box full of keepsakes from your summer.

8 When you travel with your family, are you most likely to . . .

A play games on your big sister's phone?

B start a family singalong?

C think of great topics of conversation for the journey?

D read a book or magazine?

WHICH ONE ARE YOU?

MOSTLY A'S:
the planner

You are a great team player and love to plan group activities, whether it's buying ice cream or arranging a sleepover. Every group needs a friend like you to make sure everyone always has fun together.

MOSTLY B'S:
the joker

The joker is the easygoing member of the group. Despite your label, you're not always cracking jokes, but you are full of fun and mischief! The joker is happy to step back and go along with whatever makes her friends happy.

MOSTLY C'S:
the motivator

Who cheers everyone up when the group's feeling down? You, that's who! The motivator sees the positive side of any situation. You love to offer advice to help lift everyone's mood.

MOSTLY D'S:
the thinker

The thinker is the quiet one. You consider things carefully before you speak or make a decision, and you only offer advice if it's asked for. Your calm attitude means you are great at helping find solutions to problems.

MY MANY moods

Fill in your answers.
Then draw an icon or
design your own.

ACTIVITIES

1 ....
2 ....
3 ....

PEOPLE

1 ....
2 ....
3 ....

MEMORIES

1 ....
2 ....
3 ....

DAYS OF THE YEAR

1 ....
2 ....
3 ....

Top Tip! You can use your mood dictionary for inspiration.

CAN YOU KEEP YOUR **COOl**?

**Are you a cool cucumber or a crazy cactus?
Take this test to find out!**

Read the scenarios below. Choose your response
and circle the face next to it. When you are finished,
count up your 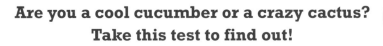 and turn to the next page
to find out how cool you really are.

1

You suspect the new girl at school is trying to steal your best friend. How do you react?

You guess she must be scared and lonely. so you make an effort to befriend her too.

You vow to do everything to stop them from becoming friends.

You don't really mind and decide to find a new bestie.

2

Your big sister is allowed to help cook dinner. but your parents say that you can't! What do you do?

Ask your parents for a compromise. If you have your sister for guidance. can you help too?

Protest and demand justice. If you can't help cook. you'll stay in your room all evening! Ha. they'll hate that . . .

Shrug it off – that's just the way it is. At least you'll get to eat some yummy food.

3

You've just spilled your drink all over your homework. How do you react?

Stand back and assess the situation. Is it too late to save your work? If yes. you can always write an apology letter to the teacher.

Rip up the paper and burst into tears.

You still feel super chilled. When it dries. it will look vintage.

18

4

Your favorite TV show has moved to after 9 p.m. and your parents won't let you watch it. What do you do?

 Ask them to record it for you – easy!

 Sulk in your room, convinced that all your friends are still allowed to watch it.

 Shrug it off – it's only a TV show.

5

You think someone has been taking things from your locker. What's your plan?

 Make a list of everything that's in your locker and check it every day. If things still are missing, you'll go straight to your teacher.

 Set a trap to catch the thief!

 Do nothing. You can replace everything, so you don't really care.

6

Your younger brother got to choose the movie – AGAIN! What do you do?

 Talk to your parents about inequality. Trouble is, you know they will still give in to the littlest member of the family!

 Refuse to join in any family fun until your voice is heard.

 Go with the flow; you enjoy most movies.

7

You want to read, but your family is watching TV with the volume turned up. What do you do?

 Read in your room, where you can get some peace and quiet.

 Decide to annoy them by eating a loud, crunchy snack and slurping your drink.

 Continue reading – it doesn't really annoy you.

8

You can't sleep because someone on your street is having a party and playing loud music. What's your plan?

 Ask your dad to politely knock on their door and ask them to turn the music down.

 Play your music loud, too. At least it will drown out the noise from outside.

 Put a pillow over your ears and count sheep.

WHICH ONE ARE YOU?

MOSTLY

Congratulations, you're a cool cucumber! It's not always easy, but most of the time you manage to keep your cool. You know when to stand up for yourself and when to take a step back.

MOSTLY

Hmmmm . . . you have a clear sense of right and wrong, but don't always go about things in the right way. Sometimes you go overboard on the confrontations, which can get you into trouble. Remember: the best results come from a calm, controlled attitude.

MOSTLY

You certainly keep your cool – you may even be too chilled. You're definitely laid-back, but this can come across as though you don't care! Don't be afraid to assert your opinion politely, or defend yourself if necessary.

MY MANY moods

Fill in your answers.
Then draw an icon or
design your own.

WHAT MAKES ME SAD

MOVIES OR TV SHOWS

1 ....
2 ....
3 ....

BOOKS OR SONGS

1 ....
2 ....
3 ....

THINGS THAT CHEER ME UP

1 ....
2 ....
3 ....

HOW I CHEER UP MY FRIENDS

1 ....
2 ....
3 ....

21

 , OR ?

START HERE

Are you a smart cookie, a running shoe, or a cute puppy? There's only one way to find out!

Make your choices and follow the arrows to find out which one suits you the most!

OR

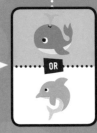

OR

OR

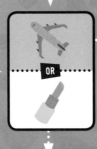
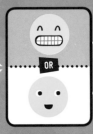

OR

OR

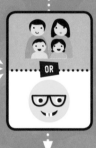 

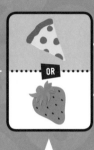 

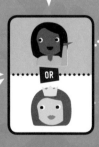 

SMART COOKIE

You are strong-minded and don't always show your emotions. You can appear quite tough, but on the inside you're warm and soft!

RUNNING SHOE

Wow – you've got so much energy! You get bored really easily and love any activity that gets you moving around. You're also a planner, and you love to try new things.

CUTE PUPPY

You are sweet and kind. You love to cheer up your friends when they're feeling down. When you're not out having fun with your friends, you're curled up at home with a good book.

ARE YOU THE life OF THE PARTY?

Do you prefer having fun with your friends or spending time alone with your favorite book? Take this test to find out!

Read the scenarios below. Choose your response and circle the letter next to it. When you are finished, count up your choices and turn to the next page to find out your results.

1 It's the weekend and all of your friends are busy. What do you do?

A Hang out with your younger sister and her friends all weekend.

B Nothing. You're super excited to chill at home, and you love your own company!

C Take the opportunity to try some new activities.

2 Your sister and her friends are joking around while you're trying to study! Do you . . .

A join in? It looks like they're having fun!

B shout at them for disturbing your study time?

C ask them to move the party to another room – or house?

3 Your bestie has a spare ticket for a concert, but the show starts in an hour and you're totally unprepared! How do you react?

A There's no way you'd ever miss the chance to listen to live music! You quickly change your clothes and beg your parents to take you.

B You pass. Last minute surprises make you nervous. You can't relax when you have to hurry.

C It's so thoughtful of your friend to invite you, and you'd love to go, but you have homework to finish, so you say no.

4 What do you think of first when choosing a new pair of shoes?

A Can I play sports in them?

B Do they look comfortable?

C Which clothes will they go with?

5 Is it important to be cool at school?

A Absolutely. How else would you get invited to parties?

B Not at all: it's much better to be your own person.

C The most important thing is to feel happy. You love your friends: who cares if anyone else thinks you're "cool"?

6 Your classmates are auditioning for a talent show. They need a girl to join their dance group. so they ask you. How do you react?

A You say. "YES!" This is an amazing opportunity. You don't even pause to think!

B You can be shy. so performing in front of judges sounds scary. You don't want to mess things up for your friends. so the answer is no.

C You think it sounds great. but you need more details. When is it? Where is it? What kind of dance are they planning? When are they thinking of practicing? What's the prize? It's quite a difficult decision. so you'll need to think about it.

7 What's the best thing about summer?

A Exciting adventures with friends – you love exploring and meeting new people.

B Summer is great. but you prefer winter nights in with your family.

C There's no best part – everything about the summer is special in its own way.

8 Congratulations! You've won a contest with a choice of prizes. Which do you choose?

A a whole summer at a sports camp

B a bedroom makeover

C a week in Florida with your family. swimming with dolphins, and relaxing by the pool

WHICH ONE ARE YOU?

MOSTLY A

Wow, you really are the life and soul of the party! You are lots of fun, and rarely let practicalities get in the way of adventures. It's great to have such a positive attitude, but be sure to make sensible decisions when you need to. You don't always think before you act, and sometimes it's good to consider things carefully before saying, "YES!" It's great to have fun with your friends, but it's nice to chill out at home sometimes too!

MOSTLY B

You're a stay-at-home type. You love your own company and can't think of anything better than chilling with a good book! You appreciate time with your family, which is important. You're also a bit of a planner, and don't like last-minute arrangements, which is why you often say no. It's great to enjoy your own company, but don't forget your friends!

MOSTLY C

Your attitude is great. You're positive and practical, which is a good combination. You like to ask questions, and you think before you act, but you're also not afraid to try new things. Your friends look to you for advice and admire your positivity. You love spending time with your friends, but you also know that it's occasionally good to take time for yourself.

MY MANY **moods**

Fill in your answers. Then draw an icon or design your own.

WHAT MAKES ME EXCITED

AT HOME

1 ....
2 ....
3 ....

AT SCHOOL

1 ....
2 ....
3 ....

MEMORIES

1 ....
2 ....
3 ....

ABOUT THE FUTURE

1 ....
2 ....
3 ....

WHAT KIND OF friend ARE YOU?

Are you there to offer a shoulder to cry on? Do you spring into action with plans and ideas for solving problems?

✓ your top eight activities, and count up each color. Turn the page to reveal your results.

sleepovers

going to the movies

bowling

writing

singing

ice-skating

playing an instrument

reading

sports

WHAT KIND OF **friend** ARE YOU?

MOSTLY PINK

You're an energetic friend with lots of energy. You love being with your friends, and you don't need to stick to one group. You're full of great ideas and you're always ready for new adventures.

MOSTLY BLUE

You are a thoughtful, creative, and independent friend. You are one of the quietest in the group, but your thoughtful nature means that your friends rely on you. You're a great listener, which is why your friends come to you when they need help solving problems.

MOSTLY ORANGE

You're a team player and love being part of a group. You're very outgoing but love to stick with your main group of friends. Your loyalty means you're the first on the scene in a crisis.

MY MANY **moods**

Fill in your answers.
Then draw an icon or
design your own.

ANNOYING HABITS

1 ....

2 ....

3 ....

AT HOME

1 ....

2 ....

3 ....

ANNOYING CELEBRITIES

1 ....

2 ....

3 ....

WAYS TO CALM DOWN

1 ....

2 ....

3 ....

31

ARE YOU A **fool** FOR **fashion**?

Read each statement carefully and fill in the Fashion-o-Meter. For every one that you agree with, circle the number of shoes on the Fashion-o-Meter on the right. Count up your shoes and check your results!

It would be so embarrassing to wear my big sister's old clothes.
3

I don't like costume parties because everyone looks ridiculous!
2

Shopping is better than watching a movie.
2

I love to dress up for parties.
2

I'd be happy to wear anything my grandmother knitted for me.
1

I love spending all day in my PJs.
1

I'd love to have a small dog to carry around with me.
2

I get bored of my clothes really quickly.
3

If I like an item of clothing, I will wear it until it falls apart.
1

When my parents were kids, no one had any fashion sense.
3

If I could, I would wear something new every day.
3

It upsets me if someone at a party is wearing the same outfit as me.
2

It's fun to mix up different colors and patterns.
1

I think it's important for celebrities to keep up with the latest trends.

21+

You love fashion! You dream of wearing the latest looks and are always on the lookout for the latest trends.

11-20

You have your own style. Celebrate it!

0-10

Fashion is just not important to you – you've got much more interesting things to think about.

IS **fame** IN YOUR FUTURE?

Every time you answer YES to one of the questions below, shade a star on the red carpet. Then count your stars. The nearer you are to the end of the carpet, the closer you are to becoming a star!

★ Would you audition for a TV talent show?
★ Do you like having your picture taken?
★ Have you ever sung in front of an audience?
★ Are you competitive?
★ Have you ever been to an acting class?
★ Do you agree that "practice makes perfect"?
★ Can you remember song lyrics easily?
★ Do you ever practice your autograph?
★ Do you feel happy when someone praises you?
★ Do you make your friends laugh?

0-3	4-7	8-10
You're not too concerned about	You've got what it takes, so	You're born to

Draw YOUR OWN

Start with you! Think about what makes you unique, and then design two icons that best represent you.

ME

TOP TIP!
Draw around your mood eraser to create perfect circles.

Now think about your friends, family, pets, and top celebrities. Circle three 😊 🍔 🎮 that suit them best. Then think about their unique features and illustrate them.

MY FRIENDS

Name: ....

Name: ....

Name: ....

Name: ....

MY FAMILY

Name: ....

Name: ....

Name: ....

Name: ....

6

MY DREAM PETS

Name: ....

Name: ....

TOP CELEBRITIES

Name: ....

Name: ....

TOP 10 THINGS

I COULDN'T LIVE WITHOUT

Fill in the boxes with the top 10 things you couldn't live without, and then draw an icon for each one.

1 ....

2 ....

3 ....

4 ....

5 ....

6 ....

7 ....

8 ....

9 ....

10 ....

38

MY MANY moods

Fill in your answers.
Then draw an icon or
design your own.

WHAT MAKES ME
LAUGH

TV STARS

1 ....

2 ....

3 ....

THINGS I'VE SEEN

1 ....

2 ....

3 ....

MEMORIES

1 ....

2 ....

3 ....

TV SHOWS OR MOVIES

1 ....

2 ....

3 ....

39

LAUGH OR CRY?

What do you do when faced with a cringe? Do you . . .

 see the funny side

shrug

panic!

Shade your most likely reaction to each statement.
Count up your reactions and check your results!

You bake a cake with salt instead of sugar. It tastes gross!			
You notice that your T-shirt is on inside out.			
Your friends point out that you have tissue paper stuck to your shoe.			
You leave your secret journal out and catch your brother reading it.			
Your relatives use a nickname for you in front of your friends.			
You're at a fancy restaurant and get uncontrollable hiccups.			
You're laughing and suddenly snort really loudly in front of your friends.			
You're showing off your new dance routine when you slip and fall.			

MOSTLY

You're super calm when it comes to embarrassing situations, and you always see the funny side!

MOSTLY

You're really chilled when it comes to awkward moments, and often you don't even care!

MOSTLY

You can't help but panic when things go wrong. But remember: you should try to assess the positives in any situation.

MY MANY moods

Fill in your answers.
Then draw an icon or
design your own.

ACTIVITIES

1 ....
2 ....
3 ....

AT SCHOOL

1 ....
2 ....
3 ....

PEOPLE I CAN TALK TO

1 ....
2 ....
3 ....

I NEVER WORRY ABOUT

1 ....
2 ....
3 ....

41

RECORD and RATE it!

MOVIES

Rating

....

....

....

....

....

RESTAURANTS

Rating

....

....

....

....

....

SONGS

Rating

....

....

....

....

....

CELEBRITIES

Rating

....

....

....

....

....

Fill in each box and shade your rating.

BOOKS

Rating

SNACKS

Rating

TV SHOWS

Rating

ANIMALS

Rating

DO YOU PUSH THE **limits** OR PLAY IT **safe?**

Think about what you would say if you were asked to do everything on this list. Circle either:

A Definitely **B** Maybe **C** Never

When you are finished, total the number of A's, B's, and C's you score to discover which animal you are most like.

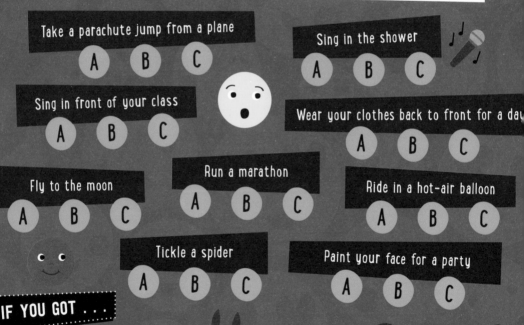

Take a parachute jump from a plane
A   B   C

Sing in the shower
A   B   C

Sing in front of your class
A   B   C

Wear your clothes back to front for a day
A   B   C

Fly to the moon
A   B   C

Run a marathon
A   B   C

Ride in a hot-air balloon
A   B   C

Tickle a spider
A   B   C

Paint your face for a party
A   B   C

IF YOU GOT . . .

MOSTLY **A**

You are a bit of a daredevil! You are first in line to try new things and have already checked a few things off of your bucket list. Just remember to share your spotlight sometimes.

MOSTLY **B**

Your balanced attitude keeps you grounded, and you're sensible with your decisions. Just remember not to be too fearful – embrace your opportunities!

MOSTLY **C**

You prefer to stand in the background and watch the fun. You are wise and not easily influenced by friends. But try to remember that it can be good to try new things.

44

MY mood JOURNAL

Fill in these pages with your thoughts and moods for a whole year. Remember to record and illustrate your amazing moments too!

	Date	Mood	Weather	Events			
Monday	20th April						

	Date	Mood	Weather	Events			
Monday							
Tuesday							
Wednesday							
Thursday							
Friday							
Saturday							
Sunday							

	Date	Mood	Weather	Events			
Monday							
Tuesday							
Wednesday							
Thursday							
Friday							
Saturday							
Sunday							

	Date	Mood	Weather	Events			
Monday							
Tuesday							
Wednesday							
Thursday							
Friday							
Saturday							
Sunday							

	Date	Mood	Weather	Events			
Monday							
Tuesday							
Wednesday							
Thursday							
Friday							
Saturday							
Sunday							

	Date	Mood	Weather	Events			
Monday							
Tuesday							
Wednesday							
Thursday							
Friday							
Saturday							
Sunday							

AMAZING MOMENTS

1 ....

2 ....

3 ....

Draw your mood for each moment:

1   2   3

	Date	Mood	Weather	Events			
Monday							
Tuesday							
Wednesday							
Thursday							
Friday							
Saturday							
Sunday							

	Date	Mood	Weather	Events			
Monday							
Tuesday							
Wednesday							
Thursday							
Friday							
Saturday							
Sunday							

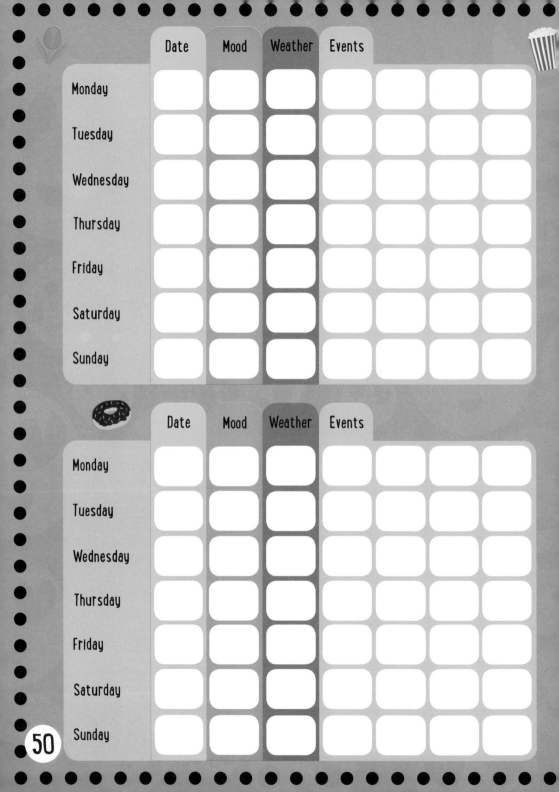

	Date	Mood	Weather	Events			
Monday							
Tuesday							
Wednesday							
Thursday							
Friday							
Saturday							
Sunday							

	Date	Mood	Weather	Events			
Monday							
Tuesday							
Wednesday							
Thursday							
Friday							
Saturday							
Sunday							

50

	Date	Mood	Weather	Events			
Monday							
Tuesday							
Wednesday							
Thursday							
Friday							
Saturday							
Sunday							

😍 AMAZING **MOMENTS**

1 ....

2 ....

3 ....

Draw your mood for each moment:

1   2   3

	Date	Mood	Weather	Events			
Monday							
Tuesday							
Wednesday							
Thursday							
Friday							
Saturday							
Sunday							

	Date	Mood	Weather	Events			
Monday							
Tuesday							
Wednesday							
Thursday							
Friday							
Saturday							
Sunday							

	Date	Mood	Weather	Events			
Monday							
Tuesday							
Wednesday							
Thursday							
Friday							
Saturday							
Sunday							

	Date	Mood	Weather	Events			
Monday							
Tuesday							
Wednesday							
Thursday							
Friday							
Saturday							
Sunday							

53

	Date	Mood	Weather	Events			
Monday							
Tuesday							
Wednesday							
Thursday							
Friday							
Saturday							
Sunday							

AMAZING MOMENTS

1 ....

2 ....

3 ....

Draw your mood for each moment:

1   2   3

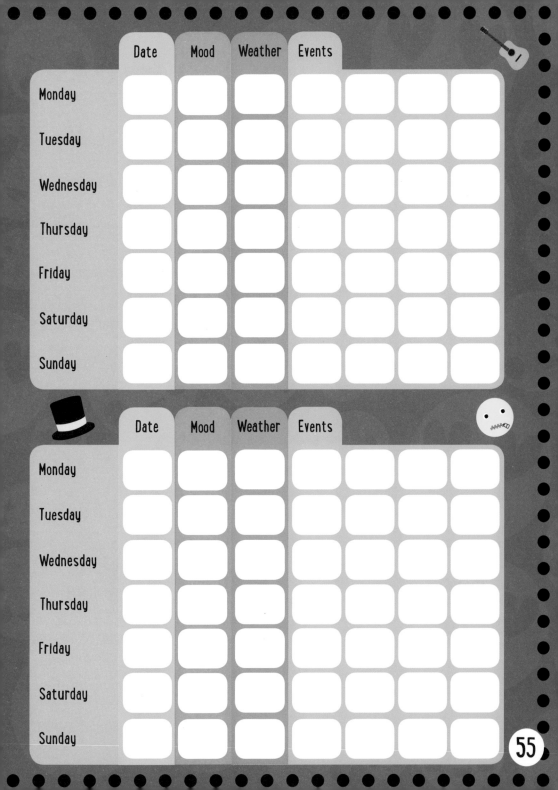

	Date	Mood	Weather	Events			
Monday							
Tuesday							
Wednesday							
Thursday							
Friday							
Saturday							
Sunday							

	Date	Mood	Weather	Events			
Monday							
Tuesday							
Wednesday							
Thursday							
Friday							
Saturday							
Sunday							

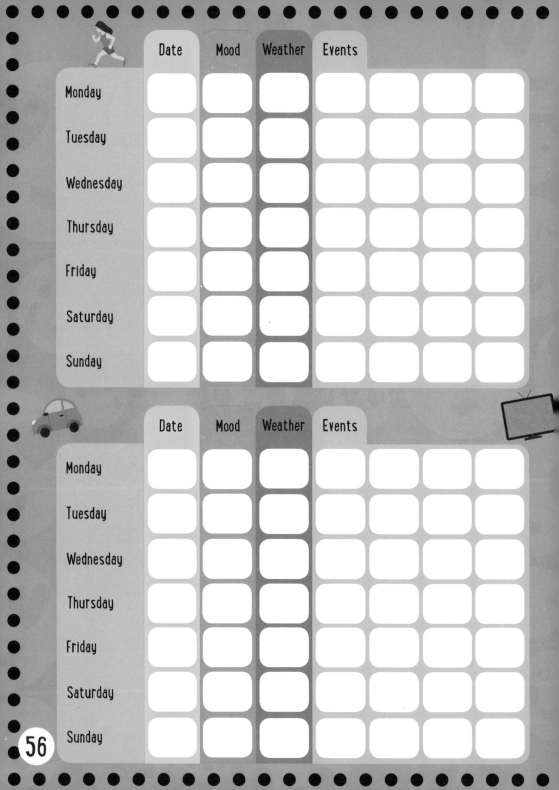

	Date	Mood	Weather	Events			
Monday							
Tuesday							
Wednesday							
Thursday							
Friday							
Saturday							
Sunday							

	Date	Mood	Weather	Events			
Monday							
Tuesday							
Wednesday							
Thursday							
Friday							
Saturday							
Sunday							

56

	Date	Mood	Weather	Events			
Monday							
Tuesday							
Wednesday							
Thursday							
Friday							
Saturday							
Sunday							

AMAZING MOMENTS

1 ....

2 ....

3 ....

Draw your mood for each moment:

1   2   3

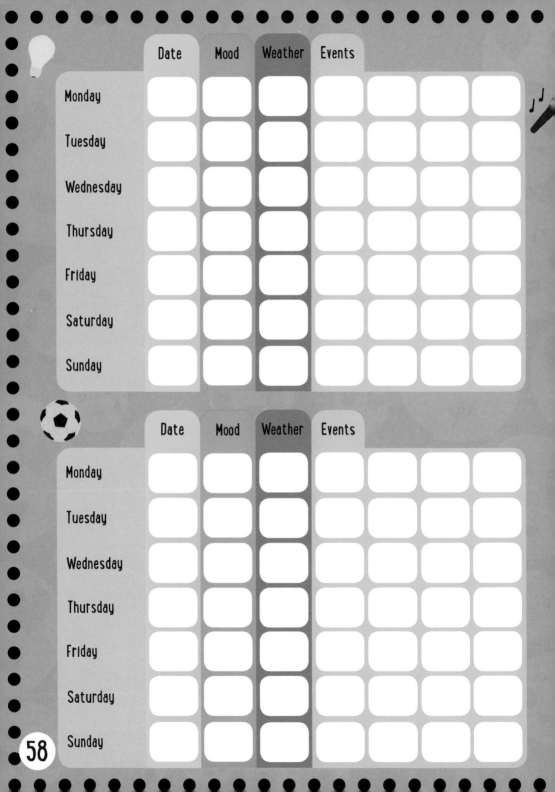

	Date	Mood	Weather	Events			
Monday							
Tuesday							
Wednesday							
Thursday							
Friday							
Saturday							
Sunday							

	Date	Mood	Weather	Events			
Monday							
Tuesday							
Wednesday							
Thursday							
Friday							
Saturday							
Sunday							

	Date	Mood	Weather	Events			
Monday							
Tuesday							
Wednesday							
Thursday							
Friday							
Saturday							
Sunday							

	Date	Mood	Weather	Events			
Monday							
Tuesday							
Wednesday							
Thursday							
Friday							
Saturday							
Sunday							

	Date	Mood	Weather	Events			
Monday							
Tuesday							
Wednesday							
Thursday							
Friday							
Saturday							
Sunday							

AMAZING MOMENTS

1 ....

2 ....

3 ....

Draw your mood for each moment:

1   **2**   **3**

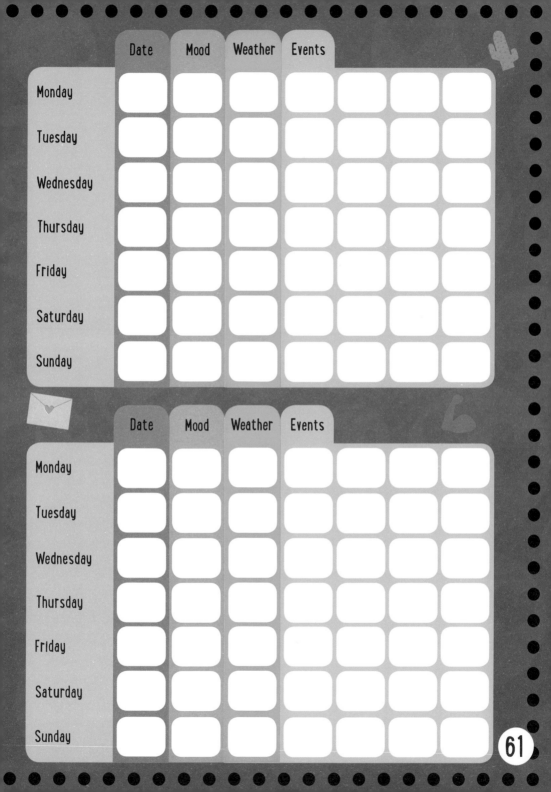

	Date	Mood	Weather	Events			
Monday							
Tuesday							
Wednesday							
Thursday							
Friday							
Saturday							
Sunday							

	Date	Mood	Weather	Events			
Monday							
Tuesday							
Wednesday							
Thursday							
Friday							
Saturday							
Sunday							

61

	Date	Mood	Weather	Events			
Monday							
Tuesday							
Wednesday							
Thursday							
Friday							
Saturday							
Sunday							

	Date	Mood	Weather	Events			
Monday							
Tuesday							
Wednesday							
Thursday							
Friday							
Saturday							
Sunday							

	Date	Mood	Weather	Events			
Monday							
Tuesday							
Wednesday							
Thursday							
Friday							
Saturday							
Sunday							

AMAZING MOMENTS

1 ....

2 ....

3 ....

Draw your mood for each moment:

1   2   3

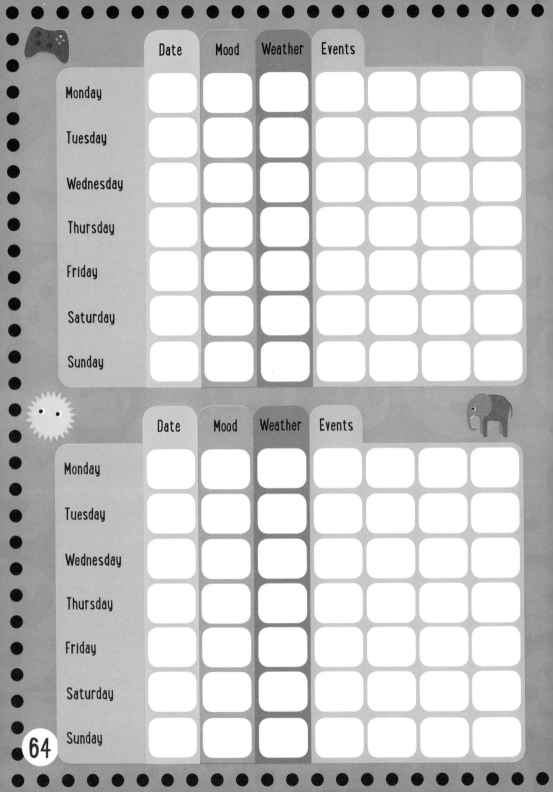

	Date	Mood	Weather	Events			
Monday							
Tuesday							
Wednesday							
Thursday							
Friday							
Saturday							
Sunday							

	Date	Mood	Weather	Events			
Monday							
Tuesday							
Wednesday							
Thursday							
Friday							
Saturday							
Sunday							

	Date	Mood	Weather	Events			
Monday							
Tuesday							
Wednesday							
Thursday							
Friday							
Saturday							
Sunday							

	Date	Mood	Weather	Events			
Monday							
Tuesday							
Wednesday							
Thursday							
Friday							
Saturday							
Sunday							

	Date	Mood	Weather	Events			
Monday							
Tuesday							
Wednesday							
Thursday							
Friday							
Saturday							
Sunday							

AMAZING MOMENTS

1 ....

2 ....

3 ....

Draw your mood for each moment:

1　　　2　　　3

	Date	Mood	Weather	Events			
Monday							
Tuesday							
Wednesday							
Thursday							
Friday							
Saturday							
Sunday							

	Date	Mood	Weather	Events			
Monday							
Tuesday							
Wednesday							
Thursday							
Friday							
Saturday							
Sunday							

	Date	Mood	Weather	Events			
Monday							
Tuesday							
Wednesday							
Thursday							
Friday							
Saturday							
Sunday							

	Date	Mood	Weather	Events			
Monday							
Tuesday							
Wednesday							
Thursday							
Friday							
Saturday							
Sunday							

	Date	Mood	Weather	Events			
Monday							
Tuesday							
Wednesday							
Thursday							
Friday							
Saturday							
Sunday							

 AMAZING MOMENTS

1 ....

2 ....

3 ....

Draw your mood for each moment:

1   2   3

	Date	Mood	Weather	Events			
Monday							
Tuesday							
Wednesday							
Thursday							
Friday							
Saturday							
Sunday							

	Date	Mood	Weather	Events			
Monday							
Tuesday							
Wednesday							
Thursday							
Friday							
Saturday							
Sunday							

	Date	Mood	Weather	Events			
Monday							
Tuesday							
Wednesday							
Thursday							
Friday							
Saturday							
Sunday							

	Date	Mood	Weather	Events			
Monday							
Tuesday							
Wednesday							
Thursday							
Friday							
Saturday							
Sunday							

71

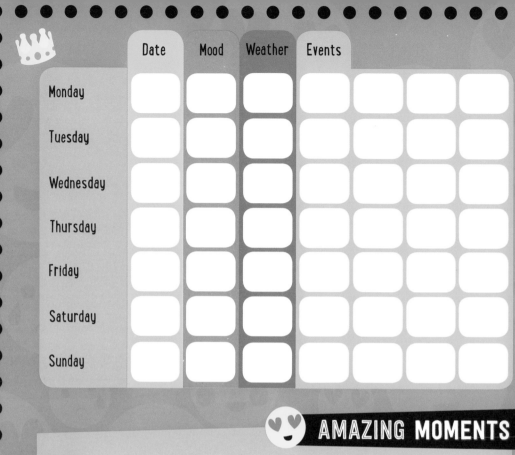

	Date	Mood	Weather	Events			
Monday							
Tuesday							
Wednesday							
Thursday							
Friday							
Saturday							
Sunday							

AMAZING MOMENTS

1 ....
2 ....
3 ....

Draw your mood for each moment:

1   2   3

72

	Date	Mood	Weather	Events			
Monday							
Tuesday							
Wednesday							
Thursday							
Friday							
Saturday							
Sunday							

	Date	Mood	Weather	Events			
Monday							
Tuesday							
Wednesday							
Thursday							
Friday							
Saturday							
Sunday							

	Date	Mood	Weather	Events			
Monday							
Tuesday							
Wednesday							
Thursday							
Friday							
Saturday							
Sunday							

	Date	Mood	Weather	Events			
Monday							
Tuesday							
Wednesday							
Thursday							
Friday							
Saturday							
Sunday							

	Date	Mood	Weather	Events			
Monday							
Tuesday							
Wednesday							
Thursday							
Friday							
Saturday							
Sunday							

AMAZING MOMENTS

1 ....
2 ....
3 ....

Draw your mood for each moment:

1   2   3

75

	Date	Mood	Weather	Events			
Monday							
Tuesday							
Wednesday							
Thursday							
Friday							
Saturday							
Sunday							

	Date	Mood	Weather	Events			
Monday							
Tuesday							
Wednesday							
Thursday							
Friday							
Saturday							
Sunday							

My top moods:

1

2

3